BUILT FOR MORE

The Entrepreneur's Guide to Reinventing Life After 30

STEPHANIE WILLIAMS, MBA

FOUNDER OF BOOKED & BRANDED

PUBLISHING

Published by Booked & Branded Publishing

ISBN: 978-1-969369-13-1

Dedication

For every dreamer who thought it was too late
This is proof that you are, and always will be,
built for more.

About the Author

Stephanie Williams is the founder and CEO of Booked & Branded Publishing, where she helps authors, professionals, and entrepreneurs transform their ideas into powerful books and profitable brands. Stephanie built a business and then encouraged people of all ages to build a life and business they enjoy.

Her approach is straightforward, no-fluff, and rooted in real-world experience. She has coached and published voices from all walks of life, proving that with the right strategy and mindset, anyone can shift from being stuck in the 9–5 grind to creating a business and a legacy that lasts.

Stephanie is passionate about empowering entrepreneurs to see their worth, share their stories, and build businesses that provide freedom, impact, and generational wealth.

When she's not coaching or publishing, Stephanie can be found brainstorming big ideas, mentoring new entrepreneurs, or enjoying time with her family.

Connect with Stephanie:
www.bookedandbrandedpublishing.com
hello@bookedandbrandedpublishing.com

Table of Contents

Introduction

The world taught us to get a good job, show up on time, work hard, and collect a paycheck. For years, maybe decades, that's what you've done. And maybe it worked — for a while. But deep down, you know something: the job alone isn't enough.

You were built for more.

This book is not about glorifying overnight success or chasing shiny objects. It's about calling out the truth: if you stay stuck in a 9–5 mindset, your life will always belong to someone else's schedule, someone else's goals, and someone else's dream. Entrepreneurship is the shift that puts your life back in your hands.

And here's the part no one tells you: you don't need to be 25, tech-savvy, or sitting on a pile of cash to make it happen. If you're in your 30s, 40s, 50s, or even 60s, you have an advantage. You've lived more life. You've learned how to survive storms, handle responsibility, and bounce back when things don't go your way. Those lessons are your greatest entrepreneurial assets.

This isn't a book about risky startups or million-dollar investments. This is a playbook for practical entrepreneurship: side hustles, service businesses, and small ventures that anyone can start — often with little more than grit, consistency, and a few innovative tools.

Inside, you'll learn:

- How to break free from the employee mindset that keeps you small.
- Simple, low-cost business ideas you can start alongside your job.
- Real strategies to market yourself — even if technology intimidates you.
- The importance of accountability, time management, and resilience.
- How to shift from "just hustling" into building a legacy that lasts.

This is not a theory. It's a wake-up call.

Permission is not something you need. Perfect timing is not something you need. You don't even need to quit your job tomorrow. What you need is to start — right where you are, with what you have, today.

Because the truth is simple: the longer you wait, the longer you put your future on hold.

You were built for more. It's time to claim it.

Booked & Branded Publishing

CHAPTER 1

Wake Up, Mentor

You've likely been mentoring people your whole life — often without realizing it. Coworkers come to you for advice. Friends lean on your perspective. Family members trust you when decisions feel overwhelming. Whether you've called it "mentoring" or not, you've been exercising leadership muscles for years.

Here's the truth most people miss: **entrepreneurship is simply mentoring with intention — and with a business model attached.** The same ability you've used to guide others can become the foundation for something profitable, scalable, and deeply fulfilling. The wake-up call realizes that you've already been doing the work. Now it's time to claim the reward.

The Employee Mindset vs. the Entrepreneur Mindset

As an employee, you're taught to:

- Show up on time.
- Follow directions.
- Stay within the lines.
- Do enough to keep the system running.

You are rewarded for consistency, not creativity.

But in entrepreneurship, the rules are flipped:

- Creativity gets you noticed.
- Initiative drives opportunities.
- Problem-solving builds income streams.

The shift happens when you stop asking:

- *"Who will hire me?"* and start asking
- *"What problem have I already been solving for free — that people would gladly pay for?"*

Discovering Your Built-In Business Ideas

Think about the "invisible mentoring" you've been doing:

- Do colleagues always ask you to edit their résumés? That's career coaching.
- Do friends rely on you to plan their parties or fundraisers? That's event consulting.
- Do neighbors call you whenever a tech gadget fails? That's freelance troubleshooting.
- Do family members trust you to help them budget? That's financial coaching.

What feels effortless to you might feel impossible to someone else. That gap is your opportunity. **Entrepreneurship rewards the skills you take for granted.**

Mentorship as a Business Model

In today's world, people are not just buying products or services — they are buying **clarity, confidence, and speed.** That's precisely what mentoring provides. Your ability to guide someone past confusion or doubt is not just kindness — it's a valuable commodity.

There are four powerful business models rooted in mentorship:

- **Coaching–helping** clients achieve personal or professional goals.
- **Consulting–solving** a problem with your expertise and systems.
- **Training–teaching** specific skills in a structured way.
- **Advising–providing** ongoing guidance, perspective, and accountability.

The beauty of these models is their flexibility. You can start part-time, test with a single client, and scale into group programs, courses, or retreats.

Expanded Real-Life Examples

- **The Career Transition Coach**: Maria was the "go-to" person at her office whenever someone wanted help to prepare for interviews. She began charging $150 for a two-hour coaching session, which included résumé review, interview practice, and LinkedIn optimization. Within six months, she replaced her corporate salary with coaching, working with just five clients per week.

- **The event strategist,** Daniel, organized every community fundraiser in his town for free. A nonprofit leader tells him, "You should charge for this." He turned his experience into a small business offering event strategy packages. Today, he earns between $2,000 and $5,000 per event and employs a small team.
- **The Tech Whisperer:** James, the family's unofficial "tech support," realized that local small businesses struggled with website updates, emails, and integrations. He packaged his skills into a "Tech Rescue Plan" — a $500 starter service — and grew a consulting business that now generates six figures annually.

Each story began with the same decision: stop giving away value for free.

The Wake-Up Call: See Yourself Differently

Most people underestimate what they already know. They discount their natural skills because "it's just something I do." But what's ordinary to you is extraordinary to someone else.

The wake-up moment recognizes that:

- Someone already sees you as a mentor.
- Problems are already being solved by you.
- Value is something you already provide.

The only missing step is ownership. Will you continue to do it for free, or will you package your skills into a business that pays and creates an impact?

Your First Action Step: Build Your Opportunity List

Grab a notebook and draw two columns. Label them:
Column 1–Problems People Bring to Me
(What questions or challenges do people consistently ask me about?)
Column 2–Skills I've Mastered That Others Struggle With
(What comes easily to me but feels difficult for others?)

Sample Opportunity List

Problems People Bring to Me	Skills I've Mastered That Others Struggle With
Can you look over my résumé before I apply?	Resume writing, LinkedIn profile optimization
How do I keep my kids' birthday party organized?	Event planning, scheduling, and budget management
My laptop is running slow—can you fix it?	Tech troubleshooting, basic software repairs
I hate managing my budget—can you help me?	Personal finance management, Excel spreadsheets
How do you stay consistent with your goals?	Time management, accountability systems

Now, figure it out. For example:

- Résumé help → Career coaching service.
- Party planning → Event consulting.
- Tech troubleshooting → Freelance IT support.
- Budget management → Personal finance coaching.
- Time management → Productivity coaching.

Circle the **three that excite you the most**. These are your starter business ideas. They don't have to be perfect — they need to show you that you already have skills people value enough to pay for.

Mentor-to-CEO Shift

From this point forward, stop saying:

- *"I just help sometimes."*
- *"I'm not an expert."*
- *"It's not really a business."*

Instead, start affirming:

- *"I guide people to results."*
- *"My skills create value."*
- *"I'm building a business that changes lives — starting with mine."*

This is not about inflating your ego. It's about owning your impact. You're not "just" a mentor. You are a leader in the making. And leaders build legacies.

Key Takeaway: The wake-up call is not about learning something new — it's about recognizing the value you already carry and daring to monetize it.

CHAPTER 2

Restructured but Not Ruined

L ife after a layoff, demotion, or "corporate restructuring" can feel like free-fall. Suddenly, your calendar is blank where it once dictated your location. The direct deposit that arrived like clockwork... stops. The identity you tied to a job title feels stripped away.

But here's the truth: **restructures don't end you — they reveal you.** They peel back the illusion of stability and force you to see what has always been true: your value does not vanish when a role disappears.

This chapter is your reframe. Instead of asking, *"Who will hire me now?"* the better question is:

"Which problem can I solve, and who will pay me for it?"

That shift is the birth of your business.

Your value didn't vanish — your context did

Companies pay you for a sliver of your capabilities. When the role ends, your skills remain intact. The layoff didn't erase your ability to lead a team, handle a crisis, design a process, or close a sale.

The challenge is learning how to **monetize those abilities on their own terms.**

Ask yourself:

- Which problems have I repeatedly solved in past roles?
- What outcomes did those solutions create?
- Who outside of my old company would also pay for those results?

When you stop tying your identity to a company name and start anchoring it to the results you can deliver, you shift from *displaced employee* to *emerging entrepreneur.*

The Skills-to-Service Method

Here's a framework for translating your professional history into marketable offers.

Step 1: Skills Inventory (10 minutes)

List 10 asks people consistently trusted you with. Don't sanitize or downplay. Include things like:

- Calming angry customers
- Making sense of messy spreadsheets
- Training new hires
- Writing emails that actually got replies
- Creating schedules that kept chaos under control

Step 2: Results Inventory (10 minutes)

For each skill, list the outcome you produced:

- "Recovered $18,000 in unpaid invoices,"
- "Cut onboarding time from 6 weeks to 3."
- "Kept 3 key clients from canceling."
- "Boosted sales calls by 40% through better scripts."

Step 3: Translate to Offers (10 minutes)

Turn each result into a service:

- "Collections follow-up sprint for small businesses,"
- "Onboarding redesign package."
- "Customer retention recovery plan."
- "Sales call optimization workshop."

This simple exercise proves that you are not starting from zero. You are starting with a proof.

Mapping Experience Into Business Lanes

Here are common categories where ex-employees often find opportunity:

- **Operations** → workflow cleanups, SOP writing, light project management
- **Customer Service** → service recovery training, mystery shopper audits, inbox support
- **Marketing/Admin** → newsletters, social captions, scheduling, CRM clean-ups
- **People Leadership** → hiring kits, interview scorecards, team launch playbooks

Pick one lane to focus on for the next 90 days. Not forever — just long enough to generate proof, confidence, and revenue.

The 30-Day Stabilize & Sell Plan

When income shocks hit, you don't need a five-year plan. You need oxygen, cash flow and clarity.

Week 1: Foundation
- Register your business name (or operate under your own name).
- Open a separate business bank account (even a free option).
- Write a one-page offer: who it's for, what's included, price, and start date.

Week 2: Pipeline
- Make a list of 40 warm contacts (former colleagues, vendors, friends who know your work).
- Send a reconnection note:
  "Hey [Name], quick update — I'm now offering [result] for [who]. I'm taking on 3 pilot clients this month at [$X]. Want details?"
- Post one credibility story on your main social platform.

Week 3: Delivery
- Land 1–3 pilot clients at a "swift start" price (not free).
- Over deliver on results.
- At the end of each project, collect a testimonial and offer a renewal/upgrade.

Week 4: Systemize
- Turn what you just did into a repeatable process: checklist, email templates, before/after metrics.
- Raise their prices for the next three clients.

Pricing That Respects Reality

Avoid billing hourly. You're not selling time — you're selling outcomes. Start with a price you can say confidently without flinching. Then layer:

- A **fast-start premium** for urgent work.
- A **pay-in-full discount** for commitment.

For example: "$750 per week for 3 weeks, paid upfront ($2,250)."

This communicates value and sets the tone that you are a professional, not a freelancer scrambling for scraps.

The Resilience Ritual

Three moves to keep your head steady when circumstances wobble:

1. **Name the loss.** Don't minimize or spiritualize it. Yes, it stings.
2. **Extract the lesson.** What skill or experience can you monetize from this setback?
3. **Choose the following smallest action.** Just one call. One post. One ask. Today.

Remember: restructuring isn't a verdict — it's a redirect. The job ended. Your value didn't.

Practical Worksheet: From Job Loss to Business Launch

Old Role / Task	Result Achieved	Potential Business Offer
Trained new employee	Cut onboarding from 6 weeks to 3	"Onboarding Redesign Sprint for small companies

Old Role / Task	Result Achieved	Potential Business Offer
Handled escalated customer calls	Saved $50K at risk contracts	"Customer Retention Recovery Plan
Wrote weekly sales emails	Increased click rates by 40%	Email Campaign Tune-Up
Managed shift schedules	Reduced overtime by 15%	"Workforce Scheduling System
Fixed invoice errors	Recovered $18,000 in receivables	"Collections Clean-Up Service

Fill out this table with your own history. Circle two offers you can test in the next 30 days.

Key Takeaway: A restructure is not your ending. It's your invitation. You are not broken; you are being redirected toward building something of your own.

CHAPTER 3

When Action Meets Change

Most dreams don't die because people lack intelligence or resources. They die from **dehydration** — too little action over too long a time. You don't need the perfect plan to start; you need a bias toward motion.

Here's the truth: **action creates data, and data beats doubt.**

You can't think your way into clarity. Move *your way into it*. Every step you take, no matter how small, teaches you something about your market, your offer, and yourself.

The Myth of the Perfect Moment

There will always be a reason to wait.

- *"The kids' schedules are too busy right now."*
- *"It's the wrong season for my industry."*
- *"I need more confidence first."*

But here's the reality: there is no perfect moment.

The bridge between "someday" and "now" is built plank by plank, through daily, imperfect actions.

Entrepreneurs who succeed don't wait until they feel ready. They act before the readiness shows up — and the readiness comes because of the action.

The–One–One Rule (for 90 Days)

In the beginning, complexity is the enemy. Focus is your greatest advantage.

For the first 90 days of your business:

1. **One Audience**–Choose the most reachable, specific slice of people you can help.
   Example: "Local home organizers for busy parents," or "Solo therapists needing intake cleanup."
2. **One Offer**–Focus on one service with one outcome. Don't overwhelm yourself with menus.
   Example: "Onboarding Redesign Package" instead of five different coaching tiers.
3. **One Channel**–Show up where your audience actually spends time.

   Example: LinkedIn for professionals, Facebook groups for parents, or local bulletin boards for community services.

Depth beats breadth. Doing something repeatedly is better than trying to do something new.

The 10×10 Momentum Method

If you only have 30 minutes a day, here's how to build momentum in just two weeks:

For 10 weekdays, commit to:

- **Send 2–5 tailored messages during the 10 minutes of outreach.**
- **For 10 minutes of audience education, share a tip, checklist, or insight online.**
- **Silence isn't rejection after 10 minutes of follow-ups.**

That's 30 minutes a day. By the end of two weeks, you'll either have conversations booked or you'll have real data to refine your message. Either way, you win.

The Decide → Do → Debrief Loop

Every micro-project should run on a simple loop:

1. **Decide–choose** a specific experiment.
   Example: "Pilot a two-week 'customer save' sprint for a boutique gym."
2. **Do**–Deliver the offer to one paying client at a clear price.
3. **Debrief–ask** yourself:
   - What caused the result?
   - What was dragged or was heavy?
   - What should be changed next time?

Write these notes immediately after delivery. They will become both your upgrades *and* your marketing copy.

Make It Hard to Procrastinate

Procrastination is often a systemic issue, not a discipline issue. Here's how to build fiction *out* of your day:

- **Default Calendar Block** → Add a daily 45-minute "Revenue Hour" dedicated only to outreach, delivery, or sales activity.
- **Friction Removal** → Draft message templates, keep your lead list open in a pinned tab, and pre-decide tomorrow's three actions before you go to bed.
- **Accountability Check** → Text an accountability partner by 9 a.m. with your day's top three commitments, then check back at 5 p.m. with outcomes.

The 72-Hour Rule (Non-Negotiable)

Any idea worth doing deserves at least one irreversible small step within 72 hours.

- Buy the domain.
- Set up the booking link.
- Post the offer.
- Email three contacts.

Why? Because the longer you wait, the louder fear becomes. Action lowers fear's volume.

Expanded Real-Life Examples

- **The Fitness Trainer**: Angela dreamed of launching her online coaching business but kept stalling on the website. Instead of waiting, she started with a one-page booking form and a weekly workout email. Within a month, she had five paying clients — proof that the website could come later.
- **The Local Baker**: Marcus loved baking but thought he needed a storefront. A mentor challenged him to sell 20 boxes of cookies through Instagram within two weeks. He sold out in three days and used the cash flow to fund his first commercial kitchen rental.
- **The Virtual Assistant**: Carla wanted to transition out of her 9–5. She sent messages to 10 former colleagues offering admin support at $300/month. Three said yes. That was her launch — no complicated funnel, just direct action.

Practical Worksheet: 72-Hour Action Plan

Idea I've Been Sitting On	Irreversible Small Step (within 72 hours)	Date/Deadline
Launch a side hustle tutoring math	Post an offer in 2 parent Facebook groups	[Insert Date]
Start a consulting package for small gyms	Email 5 gym owners I know	[Insert Date]
Sell baked goods locally	Offer 10 boxes for sale on Instagram stories	[Insert Date]
Begin freelance tech support	Print flyers and drop them at 3 local shops	[Insert Date]
Create my first eBook	Draft 3 chapter titles	[Insert Date]

Fill in five ideas you've delayed. Commit to one small but permanent action within the next 72 hours. Progress beats perfection every single time.

Key Takeaway: Waiting won't bring clarity. Movement will. Even the smallest consistent actions compound into confidence, clients, and cash flow.

CHAPTER 4

The AI Factor

There's a lot of noise about artificial intelligence. Some people fear it will take jobs. Others see it as a magic shortcut. The truth is simpler: **AI won't replace you — but entrepreneurs who learn to leverage it will outpace those who don't.**

Think of AI as your personal force multiplier. It won't replace your creativity, your judgment, or your human edge. Instead, it speeds up the tasks that drain your time, so you can focus on the work that makes money and builds trust.

For solo entrepreneurs, this is revolutionary. With the right prompts and workflows, you can collapse 10 hours of grunt work into 2 hours of focused effort.

Where AI Saves You Hours

Here are the core areas where AI becomes your silent business partner:

- **Idea to Outline** → Feed AI your target audience and desired outcome, and it will draft an outline for a workshop, proposal, or program.

- **First-Pass Writing** → Emails, FAQs, policies, landing page copy — AI can create the draft. You polish it with your voice.
- **Research Synthesis** → Instead of combing through dozens of articles, ask AI: "Summarize the top 5 complaints homeowners have about moving services." Use that insight to position your service.
- **SOPs & Checklists** → Document your process in minutes. AI helps you turn "what's in your head" into repeatable systems.
- **Client Communication** → Proposals, recap emails, follow-up notes — AI ensures you never stare at a blank screen again.

When used wisely, AI is like having a junior assistant who never sleeps.

The AI Prompt Framework

Most people get mediocre results from AI because they ask vague questions. A strong prompt has three parts:

1. **Context** → Define the role AI should play.
   "You are a service operations consultant helping local gyms reduce cancelations."
2. **Input** → Provide raw details or notes.
   "Here is what the gym currently does
3. **Ask for the exact item you need.**
4. *"Give me a two-week sprint plan with daily tasks, a client email template, and a seven-question exit survey."*

Always request **options** and **next steps.** Then edit for your tone.

The 60-Minute AI Workflow (Weekly)

Here's how one focused hour with AI can save you five:

- **10 minutes** → Outline one helpful post + one offer post.
- **20 minutes** → Draft an email template + landing page copy.
- **15 minutes** → Build a mini-SOP for a recurring client task.
- **15 minutes** → Repurpose last week's content into a video script.

Instead of scrambling all week, you enter with structure. One hour replaces scattered effort.

Expanded Real-Life Examples

- **The Marketing Freelancer**: Sofia used to spend half her week writing social posts for clients. Now, she uses AI to generate the first drafts. She spends her time refining tone and strategy instead of wrestling with blank pages. The result? She doubled her client load without burning out.
- **The virtual assistant** Trevor supports three business coaches. Before AI, it took him two hours to draft SOPs from messy notes. Now, he feeds AI the raw details, and within minutes, he has polished

checklists. Something that used to take a long time to do became quick and useful.

- **The Local Consultant**: Alicia advises small cafés on improving the customer experience. She uses AI to analyze customer feedback and generate trend reports. Instead of just giving opinions, she delivers data-driven insights — positioning her as a premium advisor.

These entrepreneurs didn't let AI replace them. They let it amplify them.

Guardrails: Protecting Quality and Ethics

AI is powerful, but it's not perfect. Use these guardrails:

- **Accuracy** → Verify every statistic or claim. AI "guesses" — you confirm.
- **Voice** → Read everything aloud. If it doesn't sound like you, rewrite.
- **Privacy** → Never paste confidential client data. Summarize or anonymize.
- **Human Touch** → Add a story, warning, or success example to every AI output. That's what makes it credible and personal.

AI delivers speed. You deliver sense. Together, they become a premium experience.

Pair AI With Your Toolkit

AI works best as part of your existing workflow.

- **Canva** → Generate branded layouts with AI-assisted design.
- **Google Workspace** → AI-drafted docs, Sheets for tracking, Drive for SOP storage.
- **Calendars/CRMs** → AI-generated reminders and follow-ups directly inside your systems.

The goal is not to replace tools — it's supercharging them.

Key takeaway: AI is not the enemy of entrepreneurs — stagnation is. When you pair technology's speed with your humanity, you become unstoppable.

More AI, More Opportunity

If Chapter 4 showed you how AI saves time, this bridge chapter shows you something even more powerful: **how to turn that saved time into money.**

Efficiency is valuable, but only if you channel it into offers people want and will pay for. The question isn't just *"How do I use AI to work faster?"* It's *"How do I use AI to design services, products, and experiences that generate income?"*

AI doesn't just make you quicker — it makes you scalable. And scalability is where side hustles turn into actual businesses.

AI-Enabled Low-Cost Offers

Here are service models where AI becomes your silent partner, allowing you to deliver faster without sacrificing quality:

- **Quickstart Guides**
  Example: "New renter move-in checklist," "First-time catering prep kit," or "Home declutter weekend plan."
  AI drafts the structure → you personalize it → package it as a PDF or bonus add-on to your service.
- **Audit + Action Sessions**
  Offer 60-minute audits for websites, customer flows, or service scripts. Use AI to organize findings and create a polished "Action Report" with next steps. Clients pay for clarity they can act on immediately.
- **Template Libraries**
  Intake forms, client onboarding emails, follow-up sequences. AI helps you generate polished templates, and you sell them as a bundle or include them in higher-tier packages.
- **Content Repurposing Service**
  Offer: "1 Zoom call → 10 pieces of content." AI transcribes, drafts captions, and structures posts. You polish and deliver. For busy professionals, this service is a significant fundamental change.

Sample Micro-Workflows

- **Catering Side Hustle**
  - AI creates menu descriptions, allergen notes, and prep timelines.
  - You handle pricing, taste, presentation, and relationships.
- **Local Cleaning/Organizing**
  - AI → Builds cost estimators, supply lists, and before/after report templates.
  - You → Deliver personalized service with warmth and trust.
- **Handyperson or Lawn Care**
  - AI generates seasonal maintenance schedules, safety checklists, and follow-up reminders.
  - You → Execute the service with reliability and guarantees.

Notice the pattern: **AI handles the paperwork; you handle the people.**

Positioning: Turning Tools Into Premium Offers

Here's the difference between a beginner and a legacy-builder: beginners sell labor, legacy-builders sell outcomes.

- Don't say: *"I'll manage your emails."*
- Say: *"I'll create an email system that saves you 5 hours a week."*

- Don't say: *"I'll design your social captions."*
- Say: *"I'll deliver 10 high-engagement posts that grow your visibility."*

AI gives you the leverage to move from selling *time* to selling *transformation*. That's the positioning shift that commands higher rates and repeat clients.

Expanded Real-Life Examples

- **The Small Business Auditor**: Janelle used AI to create a structured "Customer Experience Audit" for local shops. She charges $497 per session and delivers a professional PDF report within 48 hours. Clients see her as a strategist, not just a consultant.
- **The Digital Content Partner**: Omar helps real estate agents stay visible online. He records a one-hour video call with them, then uses AI to repurpose it into posts, captions, and newsletters. What used to take a week now takes a day. Agents gladly pay $1,000/month for the package.
- **The Local Organizer**: Nina turned her passion for decluttering into a premium service. AI helps her create customized "Post-Session Maintenance Plans" for each client. Instead of just cleaning a closet, she delivers a system for staying organized. Clients rave about the added value.

The Human Edge: Always Add Your Signature

AI is powerful, but it cannot replace your story, intuition, or connection. To make every AI-enabled service premium, add three layers:

1. **Share the reason you recommend a step for a story.**
2. **This could go wrong if skipped, and I'll highlight it.**
3. **Success looks like a win when done correctly.**

This transforms sterile outputs into trusted guidance. Clients don't just buy the content — they buy the confidence you wrap around it.

Key Takeaway: AI gives you efficiency. You give it humanity. Together, they create offers that feel polished, premium, and profitable.

CHAPTER 5

The Human Edge

I f AI is the accelerator, **trust is the engine.**
Technology can make you faster, but it cannot replace the feeling people get when they interact with someone reliable, clear, and genuinely invested in their success. People may admire efficiency, but they stay loyal because of *you* — your presence, your care, and your ability to create experiences that make them feel seen.

Entrepreneurship at its core, is human-to-human. Tools may impress. **Trust converts.**

People Buy People

Clients don't always remember the exact service you provided, but they always remember how you made them feel. The three traits that build lifelong loyalty are:

- **Reliability** → You follow through when others disappear.
- **Clarity** → You simplify, explain, and set next steps without jargon.

- **Care** → You notice details that matter to them — their goals, their struggles, their milestones.

That trifecta builds loyalty, and loyalty builds referrals.

Designing a Signature Client Experience

Legacy-builders don't just deliver a service; they design an experience that clients talk about. Here are ways to stand out:

- **The "Yes, And" Reply**
  Instead of only agreeing to a request, add value:
  "Yes, we can do that — and I also recommend this shortcut to save you money."
- **Next-Step Recap**
  After every call or meeting, send a summary with 3–5 simple actions and deadlines. Clients will feel supported and organized.
- **Before/After Proof**
  Share photos, metrics, or one-line transformations. Seeing progress creates excitement and credibility.
- **Parting Gift**
  At the end of a project, provide a simple bonus resource — a checklist, tip sheet, or mini-guide. It costs you little but leaves a lasting impression.

Consistency matters here. Write these touches into your standard process so they happen every time.

Service Recovery: Turning Mistakes Into Trust Builders

Every entrepreneur faces mishaps. Packages get delayed. Emails go unanswered. Results fall short. The difference between amateurs and professionals is how they handle it.

Use the **CARE Script** to recover with grace:

1. **Confirm** what they're feeling: *"You're right — this missed the mark."*
2. **Apologize** sincerely: *"I'm sorry this caused stress."*
3. **Repair** with specifics: *"Here's what I'll fix by Friday at 2 p.m."*
4. **Exceed** expectations slightly: *"I'm also adding this bonus step at no charge."*

Handled well, a mistake can actually deepen trust. Clients will remember how you made it right more than they'll remember the slip-up.

Collecting and Using Social Proof

Testimonials are today's currency of trust. Don't wait for clients to offer them — ask directly.

After a successful delivery, send a simple request: *"Could you share two sentences about your experience and one result you noticed?"*

With permission, use their first name and business name. Share these testimonials where prospects decide — on your website, social profiles, and proposals.

Social proof doesn't just validate your work; it multiplies your reach.

Community Over Algorithms

Digital platforms matter, but relationships compound in ways no algorithm can. Make it a goal to:

- Join one local chamber, merchant group, or niche meetup.
- Give before you ask — share a brief talk, checklist, or referral.
- Follow up personally with three people after each event.

Networking done with genuine care doesn't just create clients — it creates partners, collaborators, and lifelong allies.

Building Referrals on Purpose

Referrals don't just happen — they can be designed.

- Tell clients when you have open slots and whom you're looking to help.
- Share a simple "ideal client description" so referrers know exactly who to send.
- Always thank people for referrals — even if it doesn't lead to a sale. Gratitude strengthens the relationship.

Expanded Real-Life Examples

- **The freelance designer,** Amira, made it a rule to send every client a personalized "style guide" after their project — even though it wasn't in the contract. That small extra became her signature, and 70% of her new business came through referrals.
- **The Local Tutor**: Jon always sent parents a short progress recap after each session. Over time, he became known as "the reliable tutor who actually communicates." His schedule filled from word-of-mouth alone.
- **The Cleaning Service Owner**: Maya offered a free "maintenance checklist" after every deep-clean. Clients pinned it to their fridge and recommended her to neighbors. Within a year, she had more clients than she could handle.

These aren't marketing gimmicks — they are human touches. And they build businesses that last.

Key Takeaway: Technology may speed up your work, but it's your humanity that makes you unforgettable. Lead with reliability, clarity, and care. Tools impress, but trust sustains.

Chapter 6

Low-Cost Hustles You Can Start Today

E ntrepreneurship doesn't always require deep pockets. Some of the most profitable businesses start lean — often with less than $200. The secret is not the amount of money you invest, but the creativity, consistency, and discipline you bring to it.

Starting small isn't a weakness; it's a strategy. When you minimize risk, you give yourself permission to test, learn, and refine without the weight of debt or fear of failure. Many six-figure businesses began with a few tools, a simple offer, and the courage to start.

Why Low-Cost Works?

- **Less risk** → If the idea doesn't work, you can pivot without financial disaster.
- **Faster Action** → You can launch in days, not months.

- **Skill-Based** → Most low-cost hustles monetize skills you already have.
- **Cash Flow First** → Instead of waiting for a "perfect business idea," you earn immediately.

Remember: your first hustle doesn't have to be your forever hustle. It's the bridge that proves you can earn on your own.

Hustles You Can Start Right Away

Here are examples that require minimal startup costs but can scale into bigger ventures:

Tutoring or Teaching

- **Costs:** whiteboard & markers ($20), flyers ($25).
- **Example:** $30/hour × 5 hours/week = $600/month.
- **Premium Angle:** Specialize (e.g., SAT prep, ESL coaching, or niche skills like coding for kids). Parents will pay more for targeted outcomes.

Pet Sitting or Dog Walking

- **Costs:** Leash & treats ($20).
- **Platforms:** Rover, Wag, or word-of-mouth locally.
- **Example:** $20/walk × 10 walks/week = $200/week.
- **Premium Angle:** Offer "Pet Care Packages" — walks, feeding, and photo updates. Clients pay more for peace of mind.

Reselling / Flipping Items

- **Costs:** $0 if you start with items at home.
- **Platforms:** eBay, Poshmark, Facebook Marketplace.
- **Example:** Flip 10 items at $30 profit = $300/month.
- **Premium Angle:** Niche down — vintage décor, refurbished electronics, or designer handbags. The more specialized, the higher the margins.

Errand Running / Concierge Services

- **Costs:** Business cards ($25).
- **Example:** $20/hour helping with groceries, errands, or pickups. 8 hrs = $160/week.
- **Premium Angle:** Position yourself as a "Lifestyle Concierge" instead of just an errand runner. People will pay more for elevated service.

Cleaning / Organizing

- **Costs:** Basic supplies ($75–$100).
- **Platforms:** Thumbtack, TaskRabbit, local Facebook groups.
- **Example:** $100/cleaning × 4 clients = $400/week.
- **Premium Angle:** Offer "Before/After Reports" or "Maintenance Plans." That extra detail makes you stand out from basic cleaners.

Expanded Real-Life Examples

- **The College Tutor**: Leah started tutoring math at $25/hour with nothing but a whiteboard. Within a year, she built a reputation, raised her rates to $60/hour, and expanded into small group sessions. What began as a hustle became a six-figure business funding her graduate degree.
- **The Weekend Dog Walker**: Ryan began walking dogs in his neighborhood after work. His differentiator? Daily photo updates for owners. Within six months, he quit his job and grew his pet-sitting hustle into a full-time operation with premium packages and repeat clients.
- **The Furniture Flipper**: Tasha picked up free furniture on Facebook Marketplace, refinished it with $50 worth of supplies, and resold each piece for $150–$400. What started as weekend income became a boutique home goods store with a loyal customer base.

These stories prove small hustles are not "small" at all — they're the foundation of something lasting.

Action Step: 30-Day Hustle Test

1. Choose **one hustle** from the list that matches your skills and interests.
2. Invest **only $200** to set up.
3. Commit to running it for **30 days.**

4. Track **time spent, money invested, and income earned.**

5. At the end of 30 days, evaluate:

   - Did it generate cash flow?
   - Did I enjoy it?
   - Can it be scaled or repositioned?

Your first hustle is not the finish line. It's the training ground for building the mindset, discipline, and confidence that every entrepreneur needs.

Key Takeaway: Small hustles create big shifts. Start lean, stay consistent, and use every dollar earned as proof that you can build something bigger.

CHAPTER 7

Platforms That Pay

The fastest way to earn isn't always to build a website or wait for referrals — it's going where demand already exists. Platforms like DoorDash, Fiverr, Thumbtack, and Upwork are marketplaces with traffic, customers, and built-in credibility. Instead of waiting for clients to find you, you tap into platforms where they're already searching.

Think of these platforms as your **business launchpads.** They may not be where you stay forever, but they're powerful places to build proof, generate cash flow, and practice delivering results.

Gig & Delivery Apps

If you need quick, predictable cash flow, gig apps are the fastest on-ramp.

- **DoorDash, Uber Eats, Grubhub** → $15–$25/hr if you work peak times.
- **Instacart, Shipt** → Grocery delivery often pays more with tips.

- **Uber, Lyft** → Higher overhead but bigger payouts during surge hours and events.

These hustles may not build long-term legacies, but they can stabilize your finances while you build your bigger vision.

Freelance Platforms

For those ready to leverage professional skills, freelance marketplaces connect them to clients worldwide:

- **Fiverr** → Perfect for smaller, fast jobs (logos, copywriting, social media posts).
- **Upwork** → Better for larger projects (bookkeeping, consulting, design, marketing).
- **Freelancer** → Global projects, often competitive but useful for entry-level experience.

Mentor Tip: Don't compete on price. Compete on clarity. Instead of a vague offer ("I design websites"), position yourself as the solution ("I design 5-page business websites optimized for bookings and conversions"). Clients pay more when the outcome is specific.

Service Marketplaces

If you're focused on local services, these platforms help you find customers nearby:

- **Thumbtack** → Great for cleaning, handyperson, lawn care, and tutoring.
- **TaskRabbit** → Furniture assembly, moving help, errands, and odd jobs.
- **Care.com** → Babysitting, elder care, pet sitting, and tutoring.

These platforms build trust quickly because customers feel safer hiring through a vetted system.

How to Stand Out on Any Platform

Every marketplace is crowded. The good news? Most people blend in. Here's how to rise above:

- **Headline = Outcome-Driven.**
  Instead of: "handyperson in Atlanta."
  Try: "Atlanta Handyperson–Fast Fixes Within 48 Hours."
- **Bio = Who You Help + The Result.**
  Example: *"I help busy families keep their homes running smoothly with reliable repairs and clear communication."*
- **Photos = Proof.**
  Use a professional headshot plus before-and-after examples of your work.
- **Reviews = Currency.**
  After every job, ask for a review. Reviews compound into credibility.

Expanded Real-Life Examples

- **The virtual assistant,** Carmen, landed her first client on Upwork for $250/month. Instead of underpricing herself, she positioned as a "Productivity Partner" with a focus on streamlining inboxes. Within six months, she scaled to five clients and replaced her corporate salary.
- **The handyperson,** Luis, created a Thumbtack profile offering "Weekend Fix-It Services" for homeowners. His secret? Same-day messaging. Within three months, he became the go-to handyperson in his zip code, charging $150 per visit.
- **The Copywriter**: Elena started on Fiverr writing $50 blog posts. But she branded herself as a "Conversion Copy Specialist." Within a year, she was charging $500 per sales page and attracting clients off-platform through referrals.

Each story began with visibility on a platform — but they didn't stay there. They used platforms as proof and then leveraged that proof into bigger opportunities.

Action Step: Platform Launch Plan

1. **Choose one platform** that matches your skill set.
2. **Build a profile** that communicates outcomes, not just tasks.

3. **Commit to booking one gig** within 14 days.
4. **Deliver with excellence** and secure a review.
5. **Leverage reviews** to raise rates or transition clients off-platform into longer-term contracts.

Key Takeaway: Platforms are not the finish line — they are the runway. Use them to practice, prove, and profit. Once you have traction, you can expand beyond them into your own brand and systems.

CHAPTER 8

Local Services, Local Wins

Not every profitable business begins online. In fact, some of the fastest ways to generate income are rooted right in your neighborhood. Local services thrive because people will always pay for convenience, reliability, and trust.

While others are chasing algorithms, you can build a strong client base by solving everyday problems in your community. The best part? Local services can start small and scale into premium operations that provide stable, recurring income.

Why Local Wins Work?

- **Immediate Demand** → People always need help with cleaning, repairs, organizing, errands, or care services.
- **Low Competition When Done Well** → Many providers show up late, communicate poorly, or deliver average service. Excellence stands out fast.

- **Recurring income** → Local services often repeat weekly or monthly, creating consistent cash flow.
- **Community Trust** → Referrals travel quickly when you're known for reliability.

Examples of Local Services That Pay

Cleaning & Organizing

- **Startup Costs:** $75–$100 for supplies.
- **Pricing Example:** $100–$150 per session. Four clients per week = $1,600–$2,400/month.
- **Premium Angle:** Offer "Before & After Reports" or "Monthly Maintenance Plans" that position you as more than a cleaner — you're a household systems expert.

Lawn Care & Landscaping

- **Startup Costs:** Basic equipment ($150–$300 if not already owned).
- **Pricing Example:** $40–$75 per yard. Ten clients = $400–$750/week.
- **Premium Angle:** Add seasonal packages — fertilizing in spring, leaf removal in fall — to increase retention and recurring income.

Handyperson Services

- **Startup Costs:** Tools you may already own.
- **Pricing Example:** $100–$200 per call. Three jobs per week = $1,200/month.
- **Premium Angle:** Position as "Home Care Partner," with memberships like: *"For $99/month, I'll handle three minor fixes and priority scheduling."*

Mobile Car Wash & Detailing

- **Startup Costs:** $150–$200 for supplies.
- **Pricing Example:** $40 for basic wash, $120 for full detailing. Ten clients a week = $400–$1,200.
- **Premium Angle:** Partner with apartment complexes or offices to wash cars on-site. Convenience = premium pricing.

Senior Errands & help

- **Startup Costs:** Minimal — mainly marketing.
- **Pricing Example:** $20–$30/hour. Ten hours = $200–$300/week.
- **Premium Angle:** Market it as "Lifestyle Support for Seniors" — not just errands, but peace of mind for families.

Event Setup & Tear Down

- **Startup Costs:** Flyers or a social media presence.
- **Pricing Example:** $150–$300 per event. Three events = $450–$900/month.
- **Premium Angle:** Offer packages for recurring venues like community centers, churches, or small wedding planners.

How to Advertise Locally

- **Digital Platforms** → Thumbtack, TaskRabbit, and Care.com (customers are already searching).
- **Social Media** → Use Facebook Marketplace, neighborhood groups, or Instagram stories with before/after photos.
- **Nextdoor App** → Hyperlocal visibility with minimal competition.
- **Flyers & Business Cards** → Target laundromats, gyms, coffee shops, and libraries.
- **Word of mouth** → Every satisfied customer is a marketing channel. Ask directly: *"Who else do you know who could use this service?"*

Expanded Real-Life Examples

- **The Reliable Organizer:** Samantha began helping neighbors declutter garages for $50. Her differentiator? She provided a simple "Organization Blueprint" after each session. Within six months, her $50 jobs turned into $300 premium packages, and she was booked three months out.
- **The Neighborhood Landscaper**: Jay started mowing lawns with his old mower. Instead of just offering cuts, he created seasonal "Yard Care Plans" that included trimming, weeding, and fertilizing. Homeowners loved the convenience, and his monthly recurring revenue topped $4,000.
- **The Car Care Entrepreneur**: Lena offered mobile detailing in apartment complexes. Her advantage? Reliability and quick turnaround. By branding herself as "Luxury Detailing at Your Doorstep," she attracted not only individuals but also small car dealerships looking for bulk services.

These entrepreneurs didn't just provide labor — they created **premium experiences** by layering reliability, communication, and small signature touches.

Action Step: Launch Your Local Win

1. Choose one local service from the list.
2. Write a clear offer: who it helps, what it includes, price, and how to book.

3. Advertise on at least one digital platform + one physical channel (flyer, word of mouth, etc.).
4. Book **one job within 14 days.**
5. Deliver with excellence and ask for a referral immediately.

Key Takeaway: Local services are more than side hustles — they're trust-building machines. Done with consistency and care, they can grow from quick cash flow into long-term legacy businesses rooted in your community.

CHAPTER 9

Time Management for Hustlers

E very hustler has the same 24 hours. The difference between those who stay stuck and those who scale is not talent, luck, or resources — it's mastery.

When you treat your hours like a scarce currency, you stop spending them carelessly and start investing them with intention. Money can be regained. Time cannot. That's why time management is not just a productivity hack — it's a wealth-building discipline.

The Hustler's Dilemma

Most side hustlers start with limited time — juggling jobs, families, and responsibilities. The temptation is to wait for "free time" to appear. But here's the truth: **free time never comes. Make it.**

The hustlers who win don't work more hours than everyone else. They work *better hours*. They prioritize what compounds their future instead of chasing distractions.

Time Management Principles That Build Legacies

1. Schedule Your Hustle Like It's a Client
If your boss puts a meeting on your calendar, you show up. Treat your hustle the same way. Block non-negotiable hustle hours in your calendar — even if it's just 5–10 hours a week. Protect it fiercely.

2. The 80/20 Focus
Eighty percent of your results will come from twenty percent of your actions. Identify what actually gets meaningful results:

- Securing clients, not perfecting your logo.
- Delivering services, not endlessly tweaking your website.
- Making offers, not just scrolling "inspiration."

When in doubt, ask: *"Does this action create income or credibility?"* If not, it can wait.

3. Design Your Week, Not Just Your Day
Daily to-do lists can keep you busy, but weekly planning keeps you strategic. Every Sunday, map out:

- 1 major hustle goal
- 3 supporting tasks
- Protected time blocks

This way, you're not just reacting — you're directing.

4. Energy, Not Just Hours

Some hustlers sabotage themselves by doing deep work when they're exhausted. Pay attention to your energy peaks. If your focus is sharpest in the morning, use that time for high-affected hustle tasks. Save low-energy tasks (emails, errands) for later.

5. Cut the Noise

Multitasking feels productive, but it's an illusion. Hustlers who rise above learn to silence distractions: no constant notifications, no half-watching TV while working. Pure, focused sprints beat scattered hours every time.

Expanded Real-Life Examples

- **The Early Riser**: Maria worked full-time and had two kids. Instead of waiting for late-night "spare time," she woke up at 5:30 a.m. and dedicated one focused hour daily to her online coaching hustle. Within six months, that hour compounded into $2,500/month — all before her family even woke up.
- **The Lunch Break Builder**: Darius used his lunch breaks at work to send pitches, respond to clients, and post content. Instead of scrolling social media, he treated those 60 minutes as a business accelerator. Within a year, he transitioned from part-time freelancer to full-time consultant.
- **The Weekend Strategist**: Elise reserved Sundays for deep hustle work: planning content, setting up marketing, and reviewing finances. By batching

big-picture work once a week, her weekdays became lighter, more focused, and more profitable.

Action Step: The 10-Hour Hustle Blueprint

If you can carve out 10 focused hours a week, you can launch and grow a hustle. Here's how:

- **2 hours** → Outreach (emails, networking, pitches)
- **3 hours** → Delivering services/products
- **2 hours** → Marketing/content creation
- **2 hours** → Learning and skill sharpening
- **1 hour** → Reviewing finances and strategy

Ten hours isn't much. But consistently applied, it compounds into momentum, clients, and credibility.

Key Takeaway: Time is your most valuable asset. The hustlers who succeed don't find it — they *make it*. Master your hours, and you master your outcomes.

CHAPTER 10

From Hustle to Business

T he most significant shift from employee to entrepreneur is the absence of built-in accountability. At a job, you have a boss, deadlines, and coworkers watching your progress. On your own, no one is checking in. That freedom is powerful — but it can also be dangerous if you don't learn to manage yourself.

Entrepreneurs rise or fall based on their ability to remain disciplined, regardless of external pressure. No one will push you, remind you, or chase you. If you want to build something lasting, you must hold yourself to higher standards than any boss ever did.

Why Accountability Matters?

- **Without it, procrastination wins.**
- **With it, momentum builds** — even on the days when motivation is low.
- **It creates a habit that protects your long-term vision.**

Discipline is not about perfection. It's about creating a structure that ensures progress, no matter how you feel in the moment.

Building Self-Accountability

1. Set Real Deadlines: Put dates on everything. Don't just say, *"I'll start marketing soon."* Instead, commit: *"By Thursday at 6 p.m., I will post my first ad."* Deadlines transform intentions into action.

2. Track Your Progress: Use a notebook, a whiteboard, or a task app (like Trello, Asana, or Notion). Check things off visibly. Progress you can see becomes progress you want to repeat.

3. Conduct Weekly Reviews: Every Sunday, pause and ask yourself:

- I want to know what I accomplished.
- What was dropped accidentally?
- Next week, what will I improve?

These reviews keep you honest and focused, turning each week into a building block for long-term growth.

The Power of an Accountability Partner

If you struggle with self-discipline, don't do it alone. Find an accountability partner — a friend, fellow hustler, or mentor — and share your weekly goals. Then, check in consistently.

A simple check-in script could look like this:

- What did you commit to last week?
- Did you follow through?
- What will you commit to this week?
- What obstacles could get in the way?

When someone else is expecting an answer, excuses fade and execution rises.

Self-Discipline Habits That Build Momentum

- **Start your day with one meaningful task** before you check your phone or email.
- **Remove distractions.** Turn off notifications, limit social media, and create a workspace that supports focus.
- **Reward milestones.** Celebrate progress, but only after you've earned it — rewards feel better when tied to achievement.

Real-Life Examples of Discipline in Action

- **The Consistent Content Creator**: Andre wanted to grow his online business but kept procrastinating. He partnered with another entrepreneur, and they set a rule: each would publish at least one piece of content per week and send proof by Friday night. The result? In six months, Andre's brand grew steadily, and he built an audience of over 5,000 followers simply by sticking to the habit.

- **The Morning Hustler**: Liza worked full-time but wanted to launch her consulting side hustle. She committed to waking up one hour earlier each day to work on her business. At first, it was hard, but she held herself accountable by tracking her "streak" on a wall calendar. After three months, her early hours turned into a steady client base — all built before the workday even began.

- **The Weekly Check-In Group**: Three friends launched different hustles but struggled to stay on track. They created a Sunday night accountability call where each shared their wins, misses, and next steps. Knowing they'd have to report back kept all three consistent. A year later, each of them had grown their hustles into profitable part-time businesses.

These stories show that accountability is not about perfection — it's about **showing up consistently**, even when motivation is low.

Key Takeaway: Freedom without accountability is a trap. The entrepreneurs who succeed are the ones who impose discipline on themselves, set clear deadlines, track progress, and surround themselves with accountability. Build these habits now, and your hustle won't just survive — it will thrive.

CHAPTER 11

Marketing Made Simple

Marketing doesn't have to be complicated. In fact, the most successful entrepreneurs know how to keep it clear and focused. At its core, marketing is simply communicating three things with confidence and consistency:

- Who you help.
- What problem do you solve?
- How they can reach you.

If your audience understands these three points, you already have the foundation for growth. Marketing is not about tricks — it's about clarity and connection.

Why Marketing Is Non-Negotiable

You can have the best service in the world, but if no one knows you exist, your hustle won't survive. Visibility is the lifeblood of business.

Think of it this way: imagine a world-class restaurant hidden down a side street with no sign, no online presence, and no reviews. The food may be exceptional, but if no one can find it, the tables remain empty.

Your hustle works the same way. Marketing ensures that people not only find you but also trust you enough to choose you over others. It's not about shouting the loudest — it's about making sure your voice reaches the right people.

Simple Marketing Channels to Leverage

You don't need to master every platform or spend thousands on advertising to get started. Focus on a few simple, proven channels where your ideal audience already spends their time:

- **Facebook/Instagram** → Build trust with photos, videos, quick tips, and client testimonials. Consistency here creates familiarity.
- **LinkedIn** → Ideal for professional or B2B services. Share insights, articles, and client wins to position yourself as an authority.
- **Google Business Profile** → If your hustle serves a local market, this is essential. It makes you discoverable in searches like "photographer near me" or "plumber in [city]."
- **Community Boards & Loral Space** → Flyers in coffee shops, gyms, or churches may sound old-fashioned, but they put your name in front of the exact people you want to serve.

- **Word of mouth** → still the most powerful channel. A satisfied client who tells two friends is more valuable than any ad campaign.

Mentor Insight: Don't spread yourself too thin. Start with two or three channels you can manage consistently, and master them before expanding.

What to Post: The 3-Part Formula

If you're unsure what to share online, use this simple formula:

- **Teach** → Share quick tips, checklists, or short "how-to" insights. Teaching positions you as the trusted guide.
- **Show** → Pull back the curtain. Show your process, your tools, your workday, or your personal journey. People connect to authenticity, not just results.
- **Sell** → Don't be shy. Clearly share what you offer, the results it creates, and how people can take the next step with you.

Rotate these three consistently. Teaching builds trust, in fact. Showing builds a connection with others. When you sell, you build revenue. Together, they create a balanced presence.

Overcoming the Fear of Posting

One of the greatest roadblocks in marketing is fear: *"What if people don't like my content?"* or *"What if I look unprofessional?"*

Here's the truth: most people won't even remember a single post. What they will remember is whether you show up consistently.

Your first post may feel awkward. Your tenth will feel easier. By your fiftieth, you'll have confidence, rhythm, and an audience that sees you as credible.

Mentor Insight: Done is better than perfect. Consistency beats creativity. Show up first, improve later.

Real-Life Examples: Simple Marketing Wins

- **Carlo the Fitness Coach**: Carlo began posting one-minute workout tips daily on Instagram. His videos weren't polished, but he was consistent. Within three months, he grew to 1,500 followers and landed three new paying clients — all because he showed up daily.
- **Dana the Virtual Assistant**: Dana used LinkedIn as her platform. She shared one productivity tip per week and posted testimonials from her clients. Within 90 days, she had inquiries from professionals across three different industries, all because she positioned herself as an expert in one simple niche.
- **Local Bakery in Manila**: A small family bakery set up a Google Business Profile and asked every satisfied customer to leave a review. Within six months, they

became the top search result for "fresh bread near me" in their area — and foot traffic doubled.

These stories prove you don't need perfection or paid ads. You need consistency, clarity, and connection.

Action Step: The 7-Day Visibility Challenge

For the next seven days, post one piece of content daily. It can be a tip, a behind-the-scenes photo, or a clear call-to-action. At the end of the week:

1. Review which posts received the most engagement.
2. Double down on that type of content.
3. Repeat for the next cycle.

By the end of the challenge, you'll not only have data — you'll have momentum.

Key Takeaway: Marketing is not about being everywhere or doing everything. It's about showing up clearly, consistently, and with purpose. Keep it simple, keep it authentic, and keep it visible. That is how you turn a hustle into a brand that people trust — and a business that lasts.

CHAPTER 12

Outsourcing on a Budget

One of the fastest ways to scale your hustle into a sustainable business is learning the art of **outsourcing**. Too many entrepreneurs waste precious energy trying to do everything themselves — designing graphics, answering emails, managing social media, even bookkeeping. Just because you *can* do something doesn't mean you *should*.

Your greatest value lies in the work that generates income and drives growth. Every hour you spend buried in repetitive tasks is an hour stolen from strategy, client acquisition, or innovation. Outsourcing allows you to buy back your time — often for far less than you imagine.

When to Outsource?

A simple rule: if the task drains you, delays you, or distracts you from higher-value work, it's a candidate for outsourcing.

- **Repetitive tasks** → data entry, scheduling, inbox management.
- **Tasks in your skill set** → graphic design, website updates, accounting.
- **Tasks someone else can do cheaper** than the cost of your time → if your hour is worth $50, and a freelancer charges $10, the math speaks for itself.

Mentor Insight: Outsourcing is not a cost — it's an investment in your freedom and focus.

Affordable Outsourcing Options

You don't need a massive budget or a full-time employee to delegate effectively. Start small and scale wisely:

- **Virtual assistants (VAs):** Handle scheduling, emails, research, and admin. Many are highly skilled and cost-effective.
- **Freelancers:** Writers, designers, bookkeepers, and marketers are available on demand.
- **Task Apps & Platforms:** Sites like **Fiverr, Upwork, or Freelancer** let you hire specialists for onetime or recurring projects. You can test different providers until you find the right fit.

Pro tip: Build relationships with a handful of reliable freelancers. Over time, they'll learn your style and brand, making delegation faster and smoother.

How to Start Small

Don't jump straight into hiring a full-time assistant. Test the waters:

- Start with a **$50–$100 project** (like a logo, social media post design, or simple blog edit).
- Focus on **one task you dislike or struggle with.**
- Use the project to evaluate not only the quality of work but also communication, timeliness, and professionalism.

From there, you can gradually delegate more tasks as trust builds.

Common Outsourcing Mistakes

Avoid these traps that can sabotage your experience:

- **Being vague about instructions.** Always provide clear guidelines, screenshots, or examples. A confused freelancer cannot deliver quality.
- **Micromanaging every detail.** Delegating means letting go. Trust your hire to do the work while you focus on results.
- **Hiring too quickly.** Test a small project before committing to ongoing work. A poor hire costs more than no hire at all.

Real-Life Example: Buying Back Time

- **Jenna, the Social Seller,** spent hours designing graphics for her online shop, which drained her energy. She hired a freelancer on Fiverr for $75 to create a month's worth of branded templates. The result? Her store looked more professional, and she saved 15 hours she reinvested into sales calls — which earned her three new clients.
- **Marco the Consultant** → He avoided outsourcing bookkeeping because he thought it was "too expensive." When he finally hired a part-time accountant, he discovered the errors he had been making that were costing him money. The small investment not only saved him stress but also increased his profitability.

Action Step: Start Outsourcing This Month

1. Identify **one task** you dislike, avoid, or aren't skilled at.
2. Post it as a small project on Fiverr or Upwork (budget $50–$100).
3. Evaluate the outcome. If successful, delegate that task regularly.

The moment you realize how much time outsourcing frees up, you'll wonder why you waited so long.

Key Takeaway: Outsourcing isn't about spending money you don't have — it's about **buying back your most valuable resource: time.** By delegating repetitive or low-value tasks, you create space to focus on what only you can do — building your brand, serving your clients, and creating the legacy you're meant to leave.

CHAPTER 13

Failure Isn't Final

E very entrepreneur fails. Some stumble early, some later — but no one escapes it. The difference between those who build lasting businesses and those who quietly quit is not the absence of failure, but their **perspective** on it.

Failure is not a dead end; it is a signpost. It does not say, *"You are done."* It says, *"Not this way — try another."*

Failure = Feedback

Every misstep is data. Every setback is information. When you learn to see failure as feedback, you unlock its true value.

- **No one bought your offer?** Maybe your audience wasn't the right fit, or your pricing created resistance.
- **Email campaign flopped?** The subject line may not have sparked curiosity. Test a new one.
- **Service didn't catch on?** Perhaps the packaging was off. Sometimes the idea is good, but the presentation needs work.

Mentor Insight: Failure doesn't erase your idea — it refines it. Each time you adjust, you get closer to alignment with what the market actually wants.

Famous Examples of Persistence

History is filled with proof that failure is not fatal.

- **Thomas Edison** → He tested over 1,000 times before creating the lightbulb. His perspective? "I have not failed. I've just found 1,000 ways that won't work."
- **J.K. Rowling** → She was rejected by 12 publishers before *Harry Potter* was accepted. Today, her stories have shaped generations.
- **Colonel Sanders** → He pitched his fried chicken recipe over 1,000 times before KFC took off. His persistence turned a recipe into a global empire.

Their common trait wasn't luck — it was resilience. They refused to treat rejection as a verdict. Instead, they treated it as feedback.

The Emotional Side of Failure

Failure is not only strategic — it's emotional. When things don't go as planned, frustration, doubt, and discouragement will come knocking. That's normal. But here's the danger: don't build a home there.

Process the disappointment. Feel it. Then move. The longer you stay parked in frustration, the more it drains your energy for the next opportunity.

Ask yourself: *"What's the smallest step forward I can take today?"* Progress, no matter how small, shifts you out of despair and back into motion.

Reframing Failure: From Shame to Strategy

The words you use shape your reality. Instead of saying:

- *"I failed,"* → say, *"That approach didn't work."*

This simple shift reframes the event from an identity issue (something wrong with *you*) to a tactical issue (something wrong with the *approach*). And tactical issues can always be fixed.

Successful entrepreneurs don't avoid failure — they recycle it. Every attempt becomes a lesson. Every setback becomes a new play in their book.

Real-Life Example: Bouncing Back

- **Lena the Online Seller** → Her first product launch had zero sales. Instead of quitting, she interviewed 10 potential customers and discovered her product description didn't address their actual problems. She rebranded, relaunched, and sold out in two weeks.

- **Mark the consultant** → His first workshop drew only three people. Instead of labeling it a failure, he treated it as a rehearsal. He refined his material, improved his outreach, and six months later filled a 50-person seminar.

The first attempt is rarely the breakthrough. But it is often the rehearsal for the breakthrough.

Action Step: The Failure Journal

Failure becomes powerful when documented and studied. Start your own **failure journal.**
For each setback, write:

1. **What took place?**
2. **I learned something, but what was it?**
3. **Next, what will I try?**

Over time, this journal becomes your **playbook of resilience.** It reminds you that every failure left you stronger, sharper, and closer to success.

Key Takeaway: Failure isn't final unless you decide to stop. Entrepreneurs who win aren't those who avoid setbacks—they are the ones who collect lessons faster, pivot smarter, and keep going longer. Let failure be your teacher, not your tombstone.

CHAPTER 14

Mindset Matters

Your business will only grow to the level of your mindset. You can primary strategy, develop skills, and follow every checklist — but if your thinking is weak, you will quit long before results arrive.

The entrepreneurs who thrive are not always the most talented. They are the ones who cultivate the resilience, focus, and belief systems that carry them through setbacks. Mindset isn't optional; it is the foundation.

Employee vs. Entrepreneur Mindset

The first transformation every hustler must make is in identity: how you think about work, responsibility, and results.

- **Employee Thinking:** *"I need someone to tell me what to do."* You wait for permission. You rely on a boss for direction. Your growth is capped by someone else's vision.
- **Entrepreneur Thinking:** *"I decide what gets done, and I own the outcome."* You give yourself

permission. You design the vision. Your results rise and fall with your choices.

Mentor Insight: Until you step into ownership of your results, you will always operate beneath your potential.

Personal Mindset Shifts That Matter

Your future depends on how you choose to think about opportunity, fear, and responsibility. Here are three essential shifts:

1. **From Scarcity to Abundance**: Scarcity says: *"There's too much competition. There's not enough to go around."*
   Abundance says: *"There is always room for excellence. There is always space for me."*
   Competition is irrelevant when you focus on value and authenticity.
2. **From Fear to Faith**: Courage is not the absence of fear. It is action despite it. The first sales call, the first ad, the first pitch — all feel uncomfortable. Faith is choosing to trust the process and move, anyway.
3. **From Excuses to Execution**: Excuses don't build businesses. Action does. Your future isn't built by the ideas you admire or the plans you write; it is built by the things you *do* consistently.

Guard Your Mental Environment

Your environment shapes your belief system more than you realize. If you surround yourself with doubt, drama, and negativity, it will seep into your decisions.

- **Limit negativity** → Reduce consumption of toxic news, step back from complainers, and distance yourself from doubters.
- **Feed your mind daily** → Read books, listen to empowering podcasts, and learn from mentors who stretch your vision.
- **Surround yourself with builders** → Your circle is pulling you forward or holding you back. Choose to walk with those who are also building, growing, and chasing impact.

Real-Life Example: Entrepreneurs who join mastermind groups or accountability circles often scale faster than those who work in isolation — not because they learn more strategies, but because their mindset is constantly reinforced by peers who refuse to quit.

Daily Mindset Practices

Mindset isn't a onetime decision. It's a daily discipline. Build habits that strengthen your thinking the way a gym strengthens your body.

- **Affirmations:** Write 3 each morning. Example: *"I am resourceful. I am capable. I am consistent."* Repetition builds belief.
- **Gratitude:** List 3 wins each night, no matter how small. Gratitude shifts focus from what's missing to what's working.
- **Visualization:** Spend 5 minutes picturing yourself living your next-level life. See the clients, the income, the freedom. Your mind believes what you repeatedly feed it.

Mentor Insight: Your habits shape your headspace. Your headspace shapes your results.

Key Takeaway: Mindset is not a soft skill — it is the power grid of your entrepreneurial journey. Guard it, grow it, and practice it daily. Skills open doors, but mindset determines how far you'll walk through them.

CHAPTER 15

From Hustle to Legacy

The hustle is the **starting point**, not the destination. Hustle gets you moving, teaches you resilience, and proves your commitment. But hustle alone was never meant to be permanent.

True entrepreneurship is about building something that **outlives your effort** — a brand, a system, or a structure that continues to grow even when you are no longer grinding day and night. Legacy is when your work stops being about survival and starts being about significance.

The Hustle Phase

Every entrepreneur begins here. It is the proving ground:

- **Trading hours for dollars.** You say yes to almost anything that brings income, even if it stretches you thin.

- **Experimenting through trial and error.** You learn what works by doing, failing, adjusting, and trying again.
- **Building cash flow.** At this stage, money fuels momentum. You're not yet optimizing for efficiency — you're building proof of concept and credibility.

Mentor Insight: Hustle is necessary, but it's a season, not a life sentence. If you stay in the hustle forever, you'll burn out before you build anything lasting.

Transitioning from Hustle to Legacy

Legacy requires intention. It doesn't happen by accident. The entrepreneurs who escape the endless hustle make four strategic moves:

1. **Systems**
   Build checklists, SOPs (standard operating procedures), and workflows that allow the business to run consistently without your constant supervision. A system turns chaos into clarity.
   - Example: An event planner created a step-by-step system for client onboarding. Within months, her assistant could handle 80% of the process without her involvement.
2. **Team**
   You cannot scale if you try to do everything yourself. Begin by outsourcing low-level or repetitive tasks, then move toward hiring or partnering with people who expand your reach.

- Example: A digital marketer hired a VA to handle admin. That freed him to focus on closing bigger contracts, which doubled his income in six months.

3. **Brand**
   A hustle depends on your presence; a brand has presence even when you're not in the room. People don't just buy your service — they buy the reputation, the consistency, and the *feeling* attached to your name.
   - Example: Apple doesn't sell phones. It sells innovation, simplicity, and identity. That's the power of a brand.

4. **Ownership**
   Legacy is built through ownership — assets that produce value long after the work is done. Invest profits into things that grow: real estate, publishing, franchises, or intellectual property. These are the seeds that create generational wealth.

Legacy Questions That Matter

As you grow beyond hustle, ask yourself:

- **If I stopped working tomorrow, would my business survive?**
- **What can I build today that my children could benefit from tomorrow?**
- **What impact do I want to leave on my community?**

These questions push you beyond income and force you to think about *impact*. Hustle may be about survival, but legacy is about significance.

Real-Life Example: From Survival to Significance

- **Anna the Freelancer** → She started by saying yes to every small project just to pay bills. Over time, she created templates for her work, hired a junior designer, and built a recognizable brand. Today, she runs a design agency that operates even while she's on vacation.
- **James the Food Seller** → He began selling homemade meals from his kitchen. Instead of staying in the hustle forever, he documented his recipes, trained staff, and turned it into a franchise. Now his brand feeds families across multiple cities — a true legacy.

Action Step: Write Your Legacy Plan

Take 30 minutes this week to answer:

1. I wonder what systems I can build now to free time.
2. Are there any tasks I can delegate in the next 90 days?
3. How should people think of my brand promise?
4. This year, what ownership path will I commit to (publishing, property, IP, franchise)?

Then, choose one item from your answers and act on it within 30 days. Legacy is not built by dreaming; it is built by decisions made consistently.

Key Takeaway: Hustle builds momentum, but legacy builds permanence. The goal is not to stay stuck in an endless grind but to transform effort into systems, reputation, and ownership. Hustle makes you money — legacy makes you unforgettable.

CHAPTER 16

One Year From Now

Twelve months is enough to change your life. The question is not *whether* you can transform your financial future in a year — the question is whether you will stay consistent long enough to see it happen.

Perfection has never built a business. Consistency has. Every breakthrough you admire started with someone showing up, one day at a time, long before anyone else noticed.

What can happen in 1 year?

A single year of focused effort can take you further than five years of half-hearted attempts. Consider what's possible:

- **Start a side hustle** → Grow it into $1,000/month profit by serving a clear niche. That's $12,000 a year — enough to cover bills, debt payments, or reinvest in growth.

- **Turn 1–2 clients into repeat customers** → Build loyalty and referrals. Repeat customers are the backbone of sustainable income.
- **Replace your 9–5 income** → If you commit daily to execution, your hustle can match and eventually surpass your salary.

Mentor Insight: You may overestimate what you can do in one week, but you underestimate what you can do in one year of focused, compounding action.

Building a 12-Month Roadmap

Your next year doesn't need to be vague. Break it down into intentional quarters so progress feels structured and measurable.

1. **Quarter 1 (Months 1–3): Foundation & First Clients**
   - Pick **one hustle** and commit to it. No distractions.
   - Launch your first offer.
   - Land your first **three paying clients**.
2. **Quarter 2 (Months 4–6): Refinement & Growth**
   - Refine your offer based on client feedback.
   - Begin raising your prices as your confidence and results grow.
   - Establish a marketing rhythm — consistent posting, outreach, or networking.
3. **Quarter 3 (Months 7–9): Expansion & Delegation**

- Outsource your first small task (admin, design, or marketing support).
- Expand your reach: new platforms, collaborations, or local partnerships.
- Position yourself as a brand, not just a hustler.
4. **Quarter 4 (Months 10–12): Systems & Scale**
   - Build simple systems that allow the business to function without your constant presence.
   - Create recurring revenue streams (subscriptions, retainers, memberships).
   - Draft your vision and goals for Year 2.

By the end of 12 months, you won't just have income. You'll have **proof of concept, repeatable systems, and momentum** that can't be ignored.

The Power of Compounding Consistency

Small, consistent actions create massive results.

- If you earn just $20/day, in 365 days that's **$7,300.**
- If you scale that to $50/day, that's **$18,250.**
- At $100/day, it's **$36,500.**

And remember: consistency compounds. The marketing post you write today can attract a client tomorrow, who refers two more clients next month, who open doors to partnerships by the end of the year.

Mentor Insight: Consistency is the invisible compound interest of entrepreneurship. Each day's slight effort is an

investment into a future that feels "suddenly" successful —
though in truth, it was carefully built.

Real-Life Example: 12-Month Transformation

- **Maria the Side Hustler** → She started selling baked goods online. Her first month: 10 orders. By Month 6, she had built a loyal base and raised her prices. By month 12, she opened a kiosk in her local mall. One year turned her kitchen project into a proper business.
- **Darren the Coach** → He committed to post one valuable insight daily on LinkedIn. At first, no one noticed. By month 4, he had gained 800 followers. By month 9, he had a steady flow of coaching clients. At month 12, he matched his corporate salary and quit his job.

These are not extraordinary stories. They result from ordinary people applying extraordinary consistency.

Action Step: Your One-Year Commitment

Take 10 minutes to write this sentence in your journal:
"One year from now, I will have_____."
Fill in the blank with your vision:

- Paid off $10,000 in debt.

- Earned $50,000 in my hustle.
- Built a brand that clients recognize and trust.

Now, ask: *What daily and weekly actions will get me there?* Then commit.

Key Takeaway: A year from now, you could be in the same place, making the same excuses — or you could stand in a life you once only dreamed about. The difference won't be luck, timing, or talent. It will be your **commitment to consistent action over 12 months.**

CHAPTER 17

The CEO Quote Wall

S ometimes you don't need another business plan — you need perspective. When the grind feels heavy, when self-doubt sneaks in, or when momentum slows, the right words can act as fuel.

Words carry power. A single sentence can reset your mindset, refocus your vision, and remind you why you started. That's why I encourage you to build your own **CEO Quote Wall** — a collection of wisdom that you keep visible in your workspace, journal, or even on your phone background.

Below are quotes that have fueled leaders, builders, and creators for decades — paired with reflections on how you can apply them in your own journey.

1. "Start where you are. Use what you have. Do what you can."–Arthur Ashe.

Entrepreneurship rarely begins with perfect resources. Most businesses start with limited money, connections, or tools. The key is movement, not perfection. Begin with what's in your hands today.

Application: Don't wait for the "ideal moment." Launch with what you know now, and let the process refine you.

2. "Success is the sum of minor efforts, repeated day in and day out."–Robert Collier.

Success isn't a single event — it's the compound interest of daily effort. The sales call you make, the post you write, the product you ship — these actions add up to momentum.

Application: Focus less on overnight wins, more on the power of consistent habits.

3. "Don't wait. The time will never be just right."–Napoleon Hill.

The perfect moment doesn't exist. If you wait until you feel "ready," you'll never move. Entrepreneurs who win aren't the ones who waited; they are the ones who started messy, learned fast, and adjusted along the way.

Application: Launch now, refine later. Action creates clarity.

4. "Opportunities don't happen. You create them."–Chris Grosser.

Opportunities aren't handed out — they're built. Every client, every contract, every collaboration results from showing up, positioning yourself, and creating value.

Application: Stop waiting for doors to open. Build your own doors, then walk through them with confidence.

5. "Fall seven times and stand up eight."–Japanese Proverb.

Resilience is the superpower of entrepreneurship. Failure is inevitable, but staying down is optional. Each time you rise, you prove you're stronger than the setback.

Application: Track your recoveries, not just your wins. Let resilience be part of your identity.

6. "Doubt kills more dreams than failure ever will."–Suzy Kassem.

Failure gives you data. Doubt gives you paralysis. It is not failure that ruins most businesses — it is the dream that never got started because of fear.

Application: Trade self-doubt for experimentation. Even if you fail, you'll be further than those who never tried.

7. "Done is better than perfect."– Sheryl Sandberg.

Perfection is the enemy of progress. The world rewards those who execute, not those who endlessly prepare. A finished project, even if flawed, can be improved. An idea left in your head helps no one.

Application: Ship it, test it, refine it. Movement matters more than flawless execution.

8. "Discipline is choosing between what you want now and what you want most."–Abraham Lincoln.

Discipline is the bridge between hustle and legacy. Every time you resist distraction and choose long-term goals over short-term comfort, you move closer to the life you're building.

Application: Write your top priority every morning. Before ending the day, ask: Did my actions honor what I want *most*?

Your Personal Quote Wall

These quotes are not just words — they are reminders, anchors, and reset buttons. Choose 3–5 that resonate most with you. Write them on sticky notes, print them on your wall, or make them the screensaver on your phone.

Because when the day gets tough — and it will — your environment should remind you who you are, what you're building, and why you refuse to quit.

Key Takeaway: You don't need endless motivation. You need perspective on repeat. Build your quote wall, read it daily, and let it fuel the legacy you are creating.

Conclusion

Y ou've made it to the last page of this book, and that alone proves something important: you are not someone who only dreams — you are someone who commits. Most people never finish what they start. You did. And that already sets you apart as someone capable of building more than just a hustle — you can build a legacy.

Entrepreneurship doesn't require permission from a boss, perfection in execution, or a million dollars in the bank. It requires one thing above all else: the decision to begin. From there, discipline and consistency carry you further than talent, luck, or timing ever could.

What You've Discovered

Throughout these chapters, you've uncovered truths that most people overlook:

- **Your 9–5 is not the end of your story.** It may be your starting block, but it does not define your future.
- **Low-cost hustles can become high-affected legacies.** What starts small today can develop into something that supports your family, shapes your community, and even influences generations.
- **Mindset is the true foundation of success.** Skills and strategies matter, but without the right mindset, you'll abandon the journey before the results arrive.

You now hold not just tools but a roadmap. And with every tool comes responsibility — the responsibility to use it.

One Year From Now

Twelve months may not feel like much, but a single year of focused action can reshape your entire life. If you apply what you've learned here, one year from now you could:

- Be running a side hustle that consistently adds thousands of dollars to your income.
- Replace your 9–5 salary and step into full-time entrepreneurship.
- Build the first version of a brand that will eventually outlive you.

But none of this will happen by accident. It will happen because of the choices you make today.

Your Next Step

Pause for a moment and ask yourself: What will my future self thank me for starting today?

Will it be launching that first offer, joining that community, outsourcing your first task, or finally committing to a consistent marketing rhythm?

Your actions today are the seeds of your transformation tomorrow.

Final Word: You are built for more. Not just more money, not just more clients, but more impact, more freedom, and more legacy. Let this book serve not as an ending but as a beginning — the moment you stopped waiting and started building.

The world doesn't just need another hustler. The world needs your vision, your leadership, and your example of what's possible.

Your time is now. Your journey is ready. And never forget — **you are built for more.**

Thank You for Reading!

This book is written to help you see opportunity differently, step into action, and start building the legacy you deserve. If these pages gave you clarity, confidence, or even just one powerful idea — I have one small favor to ask.

Please take a moment to leave a review.

Most readers choose books based on reviews, and your honest feedback could be the reason someone else takes the leap to start their own hustle.

Your review could help:

- Someone believes that they, too, are *Built For More*
- A beginner gains the courage to launch their first hustle
- Another reader sees the power of starting small and thinking bigger

Thank you for investing in yourself, and for inspiring others by sharing your journey. If you're the person who loves helping others succeed, then you're exactly who this book was written for.

Sincerely — thank you. Now build what only you can build.

We've included a free downloadable workbook to help you apply these principles.

Scan for FREE WORKBOOK printable tracker & digital copy

About the Author

Stephanie Williams is the founder and CEO of Booked & Branded Publishing, where she helps authors, professionals, and entrepreneurs transform their ideas into powerful books and profitable brands. Stephanie, having started her own business, wanted to help others, particularly those in their 30s and older, by proving that it is possible to create a satisfying life and business, no matter their age.

Her approach is straightforward, no-fluff, and rooted in real-world experience. She has coached and published voices from all walks of life, proving that with the right strategy and mindset, anyone can shift from being stuck in the 9–5 grind to creating a business and a legacy that lasts.

Stephanie is passionate about empowering entrepreneurs to see their worth, share their stories, and build businesses that provide freedom, impact, and generational wealth.

When she's not coaching or publishing, Stephanie can be found brainstorming big ideas, mentoring new entrepreneurs, or enjoying time with her family.

Connect with Stephanie:
www.bookedandbrandedpublishing.com
hello@bookedandbrandedpublishing.com

Work With Me

If this book inspired you, then it's time to take the next step. Whether you want to launch your first book, grow your side hustle into a proper business, or create a personal brand that attracts opportunities, I'd love to help.

At Booked & Branded Publishing, we specialize in:

- Book coaching and publishing support
- Brand-building strategies
- Entrepreneur coaching for professionals transitioning out of 9–5
- Done-for-you publishing services that take you from manuscript to market

Ready to start?

Visit www.bookedandbrandedpublishing.com or email me directly at hello@bookedandbrandedpublishing.com.

Your story matters. Let's make sure the world hears it.

References

- Ashe, A. Start where you are. Use what you have. Do what you can. Quote.
- Collier, R. Success is the sum of minor efforts, repeated day in and day out. Quote.
- Hill, N. Think and Grow Rich. 1937.
- Kassem, S. Doubt kills more dreams than failure ever will. Quote.
- Lincoln, A. Discipline is choosing between what you want now and what you want most. Attributed quote.
- Sandberg, S. Lean In: Women, Work, and the Will to Lead. 2013.
- Small Business Administration (SBA). www.sba.gov — resources on starting a business.
- Thumbtack. www.thumbtack.com — a local services platform.
- Upwork, www.upwork.com — freelance marketplace.
- Fiverr, www.fiverr.com — freelance marketplace.
- TaskRabbit. www.taskrabbit.com — a local services platform.
- U.S. Bureau of Labor Statistics. www.bls.gov — employment and side business data.

www.ingramcontent.com/pod-product-compliance
Lightning Source LLC
Chambersburg PA
CBHW021715210326
41599CB00013B/1660